SERVING WITH
SIGNIFICANCE

A GUIDE FOR LEADERSHIP LEVEL COMMUNITY INFLUENCERS

SERVING WITH
SIGNIFICANCE

A GUIDE FOR LEADERSHIP LEVEL COMMUNITY INFLUENCERS

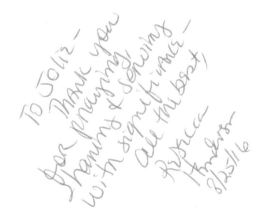

To John –
Thank you
for praying & sharing
sharing & serving –
with significance –
All the best!
Rebecca
Henderson
8/25/16

REBECCA HENDERSON, M.S.

MILL CITY PRESS
MINNEAPOLIS, MN

Mill City Press, Inc.
322 First Avenue N, 5th floor
Minneapolis, MN 55401
612.455.2293
www.millcitypublishing.com

ISBN-13: 978-1-63505-126-1
LCCN: 2016907115

Book Design by C. Tramell

Printed in the United States of America

CONTENTS

FOREWORD

A natural servant leader, Rebecca Henderson has distilled thirty years of leadership level community influencing into profound, bite-sized morsels you can quickly digest. She has thoughtfully condensed her practices, strategies, observations, and reflections into a quick read for busy people.

Rebecca moves beyond the surface level of volunteering into the depth of what community volunteer leadership is about. You are holding a carefully crafted handbook designed to fast track your understanding of how to serve your community with integrity and purpose.

Having served on two local nonprofit boards and an election campaign committee with Rebecca, I quickly came to appreciate her knowledge and experience. You, too, are about to discover her personal strengths that can serve as goalposts during your own journey to become a leadership level community influencer: Commitment to others, constant integrity, the ability to inspire passion for the cause and demonstrating good common sense.

I am proud to say that this book is the result of a conversation Rebecca and I had several years ago. We were discussing the numerous leadership positions she has held on nonprofit boards at the local, state, national and international level. Proverbs 10:14 tells us that wise people accumulate knowledge, which is a true treasure. Realizing her acute ability to assimilate and retain knowledge, I encouraged her to document the many lessons she has learned to benefit others, which is the very definition of servant leadership. She developed excellent leadership training for a nonprofit board of directors followed by the book you now hold in your hands.

You are currently the fortunate recipient of her guidance on becoming a leadership level community influencer. Read it now! Reread it when you begin new volunteer opportunities and you will be the better for it. Rebecca's experiences are varied and her knowledge deep.

This is not the last time we will listen to this consummate community leader. I expect more wise words to follow for the benefit of those who want to mature into more effective inspirational leaders.

May you reap immediate value from Rebecca's experiences and lasting rewards from serving as a leadership level community influencer.

Joy Fields Miller
Austin, Texas
Fall, 2016

TONS OF APPRECIATION AND GRATITUDE TO....

When I was in high school, Pat Wiley, a wonderfully gracious lady, asked me to volunteer with a project on which she was working. I had a delightful time helping Mrs. Wiley; she made me truly feel that my small amount of time and effort made a difference. This was my first adult introduction to the world of volunteerism; Mrs. Wiley, thank you for igniting the flame of passionate volunteerism within me. The world needs more people like Pat Wiley.

I have had many thoughts on volunteering and the work of community based organizations over the years; many of those thoughts were formed as I completed my MS in Community Leadership from Duquesne University. Because I never thought I would be sharing them, especially in written form, I do not have even a haphazard system of keeping my thoughts. I have written notes in margins of agendas, in my phone log journal, scribbled on random pieces of paper, but most of my writings are merely from mental memories. As much as I would like to, giving proper credit is impossible, given my haphazardness, but please know I acknowledge that scores of fine folks have informed my thinking and have given feet to this book.

Thank you to each board and committee I have served on; from you I have learned much more than what I have written in the following pages. It would be impossible to name every person who has had a part in helping this book to come about, so I am not attempting to try. Know that if I have volunteered with you, I have learned something from you.

APPRECIATION AND GRATITUDE

Many people have asked that their ideas remain anonymous; I have honored this. Believing the relationship between consultants and clients to be sacred, I have refrained from identifying specific organizations that have retained my consulting services.

Some have prayed for guidance for me as I wrote this book; some have read the various manuscripts numerous times; some have offered helpful words of wisdom; some have played other vital roles. Praying that I do not omit anyone with specific contributions, and in alphabetical order, please know that I especially appreciate the following individuals: Jeff Aiken, Barbara Allen, Elizabeth Banks, EdS., Patty S. Bolton, Karen Brown, MSN, RN, Madison Carr, Adam Crouch, Clotilde Perez-Bode Dedecker, EdM., Carol Dubay, MSN, RN, NE-BC, Heidi Dulebohn, MA, Scott C. Dulebohn, MD, Jennifer Gingerich, WendyMuse Greenwood, LLM, Sheri Griffin, Allen Harris, Leigh Hornsby, PhD, Carolyn

Jourdan, Carlarose Lane, MS, MBA, Mary Duke McCartt, Cookie McKinney, Douglas J. Meister, MDiv, DMin, Joy Fields Miller, Kimberley Pate Proffitt, Dr. Don Raber, James W. Robinson, DVM, Kelley Rogers, Emily Ryans, Hannah Ryans, Lottie Fields Ryans, Victoria Ryans, MSW, Cindy Torbett, MEd, John M. Wachowicz, Jr., PhD, CPA, Larae Walter, Jo Williams, and Rachel Wyatt.

I acknowledge and applaud Hildy Gottlieb for her positive contribution to the work of the world and for allowing me to liberally use the term *community benefit organization* throughout this book.

I have learned more about volunteers and volunteering from Shar McBee, author of several books, including *To Lead is To Serve* and *Joy of Leadership*, than from anyone else. *To Lead is To Serve* has influenced my life more than any other book, except the *Bible*. Thank you, Shar.

I wish to honor the memory of my great-aunt, Mary S. Henderson, for many wise words that she imparted to me.

Finally, the best for last. Thank you to my parents, John (Jack) and Marjorie Henderson. They were the best parents anyone could have. Without their support and volunteering behind the scenes, I would not have been able to accomplish anything. Even though they are now deceased, I am especially proud of them, because their last act was to donate their bodies to the James H. Quillen College of Medicine for the purposes of scientific research. What an example of volunteerism and of giving! Thank you to Jack and Marjorie Henderson for the examples they were to countless people in numerous ways, but most of all to me.

PREFACE

A leadership level community influencer is first and foremost, a leader. Leadership is a skill that can be learned; this book will give you quick tips that can be put in place straightaway. Like most skills, the more you practice, the better you get. Leadership is no exception; nor is the art of community influencing.

This book is designed to be read rapidly and for the knowledge gained to be immediately implemented. Because leadership skills are so interconnected, many of the tips tie into one other. All types of groups, ranging from informal to formal, local to international, social to humanitarian, and especially membership-based organizations, will benefit from it. While the primary audience is that of the nonprofit sector, nearly all of the tips that follow are equally applicable in a corporate setting of any size.

With the assumption that all who read this book are leadership level community influencers, I have sometimes used the pronoun "you." At other times, I've used the word "leader".

In the spirit of total honesty, have I always followed the advice I'm putting forth in the following pages? No. Do I wish that I had? Absolutely!

I urge you to go forth with Godspeed.

WHAT IS A LEADERSHIP LEVEL COMMUNITY INFLUENCER?

A leadership level community influencer is a leader, first and foremost.

Leaders give service to others.

Leaders share their knowledge, talent, resources, and time.

The more leaders share these things with others, the more influence the leader has.

Hope for the positive future of community benefit organizations gives power to current and future leaders.

So much of our attitude determines our success.

Leaders wear blue jeans, evening gowns, work gloves, and everything in between.

Anyone can become a positive and effective leader; the only requirement is the desire to serve others.

Leaders often start their influencing roles in small, but vital, roles within an organization.

Often a small role will lead to a much larger role.

We're told in Luke 16:10 that those who can be trusted with a little can also be trusted with quite a bit more.

Leaders create excellent community benefit organizations by consistently giving a little more effort.

The extra energy makes a tremendous difference.

Leaders see themselves as someone who will make the difference in their organization.

Often, just one person is all it takes to make that difference.

Leaders see that a change needs to happen; they want something done about the current situation, whatever it is.

Leaders take the steps necessary to make change happen.

Leaders keep their word; they honor their promises.

Their integrity is unparalleled.

Leaders share their knowledge with their community benefit organization.

They strive to show solutions to points of pain within the group.

Leaders model the Pearl Rule.

This rule says to treat others better than you expect to be treated.

Leaders are passionate about their association with their group.

Passion creates action.

A chain is only as sturdy as the weakest link.

Conversely, the strength of a community benefit organization lies within the strength of the strongest person affiliated with it.

The more experience a leader has, the higher the expectations others have of them.

Leadership level community influencers work hard to continue raising the bar, which benefits everyone.

The most effective community benefit organizations have leaders with a variety of personality components, professional comp-etencies, and life experiences.

The components, competencies, and experiences provide balance and needed skill sets.

Successful associations work to ensure that their leaders work together as a TEAM.

TEAM is an acronym for "Together, Each Accomplishes Much."

Community benefit organizations frequently inadvertently teach leaders things not easily learned elsewhere.

Many things learned as a leader in a volunteer setting translate to the paid employment field.

This is a triple win for everyone involved—the leader, the community benefit organization, and the employer.

If you are in charge of getting the job done, you must be willing to actually be in charge and take appropriate action.

You may very well find yourself in charge of significant change.

Changes are perceived as good or bad.

Perhaps the situation can yield a positive perspective or an outstanding opportunity.

Magnify positive changes by putting them under a microscope.

Kaleidoscope changes viewed as negative.

Neither committee nor board membership are spectator sports.

Participation is mandatory.

The more you put into a community benefit organization, the more you tend to reap from it. That reflects the words of Paul as he writes in Galatians 6:7 when he says that we reap what we sow.

**Those who run the
most efficient and
effective committee and
board meetings know
and practice proper
parliamentary
procedure.**

While parliamentary procedure can
be daunting initially, it becomes
second nature almost immediately;
it's so easy to see its benefits.

Committees comprised of effective leaders help tremendously in producing productive boards.

Many organizations select board members from effective committee members.

Value differing views and viewpoints.

You will be amazed by how much your world is widened and by how much you learn.

Something that all leaders share is the knowledge that we are all uniquely different.

Appreciate the differences in many kinds of diversities.

Leaders know there are many components of diversity.

Age, race, religion, occupation, educational level, ethnicity, culture, customs, talents, abilities, gifts, and interests are some important components comprising diversity.

Give your community benefit organization the attention it deserves.

Make sure your attention to it is with the right intention.

When you lift up other leaders, you also lift yourself up.

Similarly, when you help others, you also help yourself.

Leaders have many important duties.

Perhaps one of the most important is to try to make it as effortless as possible for those who follow them to do the correct thing.

Always take time to be kind.

It is a positive reflection on you as well as your community benefit organization.

To do your best work for your group, watch that you do not burn out.

A very effective way to do this is to guard your time jealously.

A meeting moratorium helps prevent burnout.

Leaders return to their community benefit organization with a renewed passion, enthusiasm, and eagerness to contribute to the group.

Communication is important in every organization.

Indeed, without communication, there isn't an organization.

Using the same adjectives too often dilutes their meaning.

As I write this, "awesome" and "amazing" are used with annoying frequency in both the oral and written word.

Consequently, people may not pay as much attention to sentences with these words in them as we might wish they would.

When people don't pay attention, words are wasted and meaning is lost.

Both a lack of communication and incomplete communication causes many problems.

It is nearly impossible to over-communicate the correct information.

Leaders learn, process, and remember information in different ways.

Some do this best by reading, others by hearing, and yet others by doing.

Think eyes, ears, and hands as you tailor your message for the maximum impact.

Dr. Leigh Hornsby taught me years ago to ask, "Is there anything I've not covered or that you want to touch upon?" as an interview draws to a close.

While she specifically tailored this advice and philosophy to media interviews, these questions are very beneficial and provide clarifying opportunities in a variety of contexts and conversations.

No matter how wonderful your community benefit organization is, recognize that some of your best friends will probably fail to share in your excitement.

This recognition is helpful in preventing misplaced feelings.

Leaders know that social media can be the best friend of a community benefit organization.

Used incorrectly, social media can also be the worst enemy of a community benefit organization.

Cookie McKinney wisely advises that it is so much easier to deal with the known than the unknown.

This is especially true when we are afraid the unknown is bad news.

The reputation and history of your community benefit organization are part of its culture and reality.

Stories and rumors (both positive and negative, as well as factual or fictionalized) associated with the group are also key characteristics that form the personality of the organization.

Every major event is a fabulous and unparalleled opportunity for your community benefit organization to shine like the sun on a summer day.

Minor events are also occasions to glow; minor events often grow into major events.

You may be the face of your community benefit organization to some people; they may not know anyone else with a connection to it.

Do all you can to ensure that their impression is positive.

Always speak positively about your community benefit organization.

Remember that you are the face of its public relations.

Mind your manners when you wear clothing with the logo of your community benefit organization on it.

Step out of your way to be extra courteous to people who do not know you because your logo clothing may very well be the only impression they have of the group.

Leaders are always doing something significant and positive.

Otherwise, they wouldn't be leaders.

"The people who mind do not matter. The people who matter do not mind." My great-aunt said these wise words to me on many occasions.

Leaders definitely matter; but more importantly, they know that everyone matters. Most importantly, they practice that philosophy.

Leaders make time for the activities important to them and that match their values.

If their activities are incongruent with their values, they are being disingenuous to themselves.

And when time isn't made for activities important to them, the activity really isn't very important.

Leaders under promise and over deliver on their commitments.

This creates a positive impression; it really ramps up your social capital.

Leaders have good follow-up skills and unparalleled levels of integrity.

The two traits march alongside each other.

Acknowledging your knowledge makes it more likely others will as well.

It's okay to speak up and say, "I can help with the issue because of my background."

Leaders are very vocal and proud of their group as well as the work it has done.

They share those thoughts at every appropriate opportunity.

If we fail to use and share our talents and gifts, we cheat others and ourselves.

No one wants to be cheated; most people don't want to cheat others. Leaders definitely do not wish to cheat other people.

Leaders always have time to be kind.

Often being kind to someone takes just a minute, but the results of that minute of kindness can last a lifetime.

Leaders don't make mountains out of molehills.

However, they do make molehills out of mountains.

Leaders are humble.

Leaders are very determined to move forward and keep the big picture in mind while others are lost in the details.

Leaders inspire, not confuse.

HOW TO BECOME A LEADERSHIP LEVEL COMMUNITY INFLUENCER

To become a leadership level community influencer in a community benefit organization, indicate your interest to the appropriate staff member, a member of the board of directors, or someone who is an active volunteer in the group.

Quite often, you'll find that your interest to be involved at a deeper and higher level is welcomed.

Don't be discouraged in the least if your offer isn't acted on immediately. Many things in life take time and patience to come to fruition. Wait, watch for opportunities to be helpful, and prepare to be welcomed!

When you are asked to be on a board or a committee of a community benefit organization, make sure you know and understand the expectations the group has of you.

Ask until you understand!

You learn much of the work of being a leader by simply doing the work and observing other successful and influential people.

You can also learn from the mistakes others make; this prevents you from making them.

Find someone to mentor you in your quest to become an effective leader.

Look for an OWL (Older, Wiser, Leader) to be your mentor. Your mentor does not necessarily need to be older chronologically than you, but just have a multitude of successful leadership experiences.

Perform each task or role you assume with integrity and passion.

I've observed that those with the greatest commitment to this philosophy are the most successful.

Earn your responsibilities; learn from them.

Soon you will have more responsibilities and opportunities to grow within your community benefit organization.

Work to build your reputational capital.

By association, you build the capital of your group as well.

Everyone benefits when reputational capital increases.

Using leverage makes things easier; lead with leverage by learning.

Learning happens by observing, reading, participating, and doing.

Do your homework prior to meetings.

Review notes you've made to ensure you've followed up on commitments you've made or responsibilities incumbent on you by virtue of your position.

When you miss a meeting, make it your responsibility to learn what you missed.

I've found it useful to talk to several people who have attended meetings I've missed, because everyone has a different perspective.

I tell those I talk with that I'm going to talk with some others, for the above reason.

Recognize and honor your time, as well as that of other people.

Promptly sending an RSVP to meetings and events is an easy way to do this!

Today's currency is time; people tend to quit attending meetings when they feel their time is wasted.

Many years ago, Dr. John Wachowicz taught me to ask continually, "Is this the best use of my time?"

Try to learn something from each meeting you attend.

The other side is true as well; help others learn something from you by letting your knowledge multiply.

Make it part of your personal mission to teach others.

Fully participate in meetings.

This means preparing for the meeting, being on time and staying for the duration.

Every community benefit organization has its own culture and unwritten rules, similar to every family.

You will learn these as you work with the group; the culture and rules will probably evolve over time.

So those who follow you can cite success, do what is needed to make success happen.

Just as success looks different for everyone, so it is for organizations.

Remember and recognize this!

Realize that everything you do affects everything else you do.

Because of our limited resources, we can rarely do all we want; prioritize your commitments with this in mind.

When someone asks you to make a commitment–be it of time, money, or other resources–think it through rather than immediately agreeing to the request.

This helps in preventing regrets and regroupings later.

Decisions deserve research.

The deeper the decision, the more research should go into the decision making process.

Be careful not to proxy your responsibilities and duties.

A proxy of responsibility comes in different forms, including lack of attendance at meetings. Be fair to those who helped you get the position of a leadership level community influencer by assuming the duties, rather than abdicating them.

Leadership is not a popularity contest.

Membership on a community benefit organization board or committee isn't, either.

You will have to make difficult decisions.

Some decisions will force you to confront and take action in line with your values and ethics.

A key component of leadership is forming and maintaining successful relationships.

This is because people carry out the work of community benefit organizations.

Make and maintain a list of your friends and colleagues who would benefit from knowing each other and the work of your community benefit organization.

Take action by introducing them to each other, as well as to the organization.

Constantly write notes.

Thank you notes are mandatory.

Notes letting others know you
enjoyed meeting them or learning
from their presentation makes you
positively memorable.

Create a fan file.

When others send you thank you notes or complimentary correspondence, file it here.

Familiarize yourself with the important documents of your community benefit organization.

These include, but aren't exclusive to, the budget, annual report, organizational chart, bylaws, standing rules, and the strategic plan, which should include the mission statement and the vision of the group.

When you are the new person on a board or committee, you may have to prove your credibility to others.

The quickest and easiest way to do that is by having unquestioned integrity.

Be courteous and considerate, rather than harsh and arrogant.

This will help tremendously in your journey to become a respected leader.

Some leaders rarely speak without having a good reason.

When such a person speaks, pay close attention.

Almost always, their words will be profound, important, and philosophical.

Their words will be worth the wait and weight.

Demonstrate courtesy by remaining silent when others are speaking.

No one likes to try to talk over other people.

People may not know or be able to pull facts from their memories about a community benefit organization until they need the services it provides.

Domestic violence programs, blood banks, and adult day care programs are good examples.

If you practice what you preach, others will soon be preaching what you practice.

People will be watching your actions and listening to your words, so make them wise.

Have both a bio and a resume.

Keep both updated as your role within a community benefit organization grows.

Get to know as many people as possible on a personal level.

The more people you know, the easier it is to create change.

HOW LEADERS
KEEP THE BRIGHT
LIGHT OF THEIR
ORGANIZATION
BLAZING STRONG

In your quest to be a good leader, frequently ask yourself if you are worthy of being imitated.

We learn as much, or more, from bad leaders as from good ones.

Be the person you hope others will emulate.

We grow by the philosophy we live by.

We set others up for failure when we do not clearly communicate our expectations.

Failing to communicate is a disservice to everyone involved.

An absolute multitude of personality styles exist.

Realize that traits that are important to one person may not be at all relevant to you, and vice versa.

Strong teams create and build bold dreams.

Nothing happens without a dream
behind it, as well as above it.

Pre-meeting icebreakers help people to get to know each other.

The better people know each other, the better they work together.

When something is fun, more work gets done.

Different people think different things are fun, and this is quite acceptable.

Let your committee or board chair know if you will or will not be at a meeting.

This helps in determining if a quorum will be present.

Frequently, you will find cliques within community benefit organizations.

You may find yourself in such a clique; try to include everyone, because no one likes to feel excluded or not included.

Feeling excluded and feeling like you are not included can be two very different feelings; neither are positive, nor do they create good feelings about the community benefit organization.

If you do not understand something in a meeting, ask.

Chances are good you will not be the only one wondering.

After a member misses a meeting, it is easier to miss the next one.

Quick follow up when someone misses a meeting helps tremendously in retaining their membership.

If you care about the member, contact them.

Know when to move forward and when to be stationary.

Research and dialogue usually best informs difficult decisions.

Be careful not to confuse pessimism with realism.

Do not confuse either pessimism or realism with negativism.

Do not diminish the motivations of other people.

When you think of doing this, put yourself in that person's place.

Promote and be an advocate for your community benefit organization whenever appropriate.

Resolve to be involved.

Your passion for your community benefit organization shines through when you speak from your heart rather than your head.

Such passionate speech propels your organization forward, and encourages growth.

Sometimes silence encourages the status quo, rather than steps that promote growth.

Select several trusted leaders to form your personal executive committee.

These individuals let you bounce ideas off them and are brutally honest in giving you their opinions, suggestions, and advice.

They hold you accountable and let you know when you are about to do something you will regret.

Often the least that can be done about a situation is to pray.

Fortunately, it is also often the most that can be done.

We only make progress if we are willing to make mistakes.

We learn from our mistakes, and so will other leaders.

We will also learn from the mistakes others make.

The strategic plan outlines the goals and the actions to take to achieve the goals of your community benefit organization.

The strategic plan forces the group to FOCUS, which is an acronym for "Follow On Course Until Successful."

The mission statement tells why your community benefit organization exists.

A good mission statement creates excitement.

The vision states the boldest dreams of your community benefit organization.

Like a good mission statement, the vision should also generate enthusiasm and feelings of eager, positive anticipation for making the community a better place.

Burnout spreads like wildfire throughout community benefit organizations.

Work rapidly to prevent or contain it.

When leaders feel appreciated, they are much less likely to feel burnout.

The opposite is also true.

When you sense someone is burning out, ask him or her, "What can I do for you?"

Applauding each accomplishment, however small, goes many miles in preventing burnout.

Sometimes accomplishments that seem small are actually very large, and vice versa.

Handwritten notes to other leaders are an easy way to convey appreciation.

They also grow your social capital exponentially.

Feelings are sometimes fragile and can be hurt if their owner is the last to know something.

Keep everyone involved in the information loop, even if they are on the periphery of the group.

This prevents misplaced feelings and rumors.

You may slip, or you may sit, but whatever you do, do not quit in your quest to become a leader.

Progress takes time and patience!

Change is easiest when the current reality is more painful and pitiful than the forthcoming change.

Leaders navigate waters, be they clear or murky.

One person - one leader - can create positive changes for a community benefit organization.

Quite often, one dedicated and persistent leader is all it takes.

I leave you with the challenge, opportunity, and the charge to be that change.

CONCLUSION

We find the importance of life in the lives of those we touch. Others who follow us are moved by the tracks we leave behind. Leadership level community influencers make life better and easier for those who follow in our footsteps by providing a clear pathway. All kinds of leaders make a difference in their communities, one person at a time. We can make community benefit organizations change one hour at a time. The concept of volunteerism at its very roots is changing the community and the world in which we live. Changing the landscape can be difficult. I wish you Godspeed on your journey in facilitating and creating positive community change.

AFTERWORD

I hope and pray this book has been helpful to you and your community of influencers. Based on my experiences as a leadership level community influencer, it is my fervent hope that you have enjoyed it and found the information useful, practical, and ready for immediate application.

I'd love to hear from you as you travel the path of being a leadership level community influencer. I'm looking for examples of concepts and ideas to put forth in any future books about the topic. If you are willing to share any stories, please feel free to contact me at rebeccahenderson@strategicprioritiesconsulting.com. If I use your thoughts, I will acknowledge you. Many advance thanks!

Rebecca Henderson
P.O. Box 3826 CRS
Johnson City, Tennessee 37602-3826
rebeccahenderson@strategicprioritiesconsulting.com